Numbers

**Illustrator
Sonia Canals**

Consultants
Penny Coltman
and Jayne Greenwood

one

1
2
3
4
5
6
7
8
9
10

two

2

1
2
3
4
5
6
7
8
9
10

three

3

1
2
3
4
5
6
7
8
9
10

1
2
3
4
5
6
7
8
9
10

four

five

5

1 2 3 4 5 6 7 8 9 10

1
2
3
4
5
6
7
8
9
10

six

6

1
2
3
4
5
6
7
8
9
10

Seven

7

1
2
3
4
5
6
7
8
9
10

eight

8

1 2 3 4 5 6 7 8 9 10

1
2
3
4
5
6
7
8
9
10

nine

1
2
3
4
5
6
7
8
9
10

ten

1
2
3
4
5
6
7
8
9
10

1
2
3
4
5
6
7
8
9
10

5 10

1
2
3
4
5
6
7
8
9
10

bye bye!

.... Notes for Parents

Using This Book

Explanation

This book will help you to introduce your child to the world of numbers and counting. Children become ready to learn about using numbers at different ages.

Whatever stage your child is at, using this book together will be an enjoyable and rewarding experience.

Sharing this book should be seen as fun. Choose a time when both you and your child feel relaxed and comfortable.

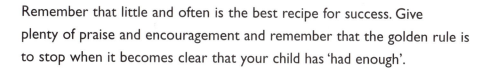

Remember that little and often is the best recipe for success. Give plenty of praise and encouragement and remember that the golden rule is to stop when it becomes clear that your child has 'had enough'.

With your child

- Look at the cover of the book together. Talk about any numbers you can see.
- Explain that this is a book about numbers and counting. On every page you will find a hand with fingers to count. Encourage your child to spot these on each page.
- As you look through the pages chat about the pictures you see, recognising familiar objects and helping your child to learn about some new ones.

notes

Counting

Explanation

Learning to count is not as easy as it first seems. There are several skills which children need to master.

The first step is for your child to learn the string of number words, starting with the numbers from one to five, and then on to ten.

The next important stage is to learn that when you are counting, each object is given one counting word, or number. This is called one-to-one matching. Sometimes children need help in 'keeping count', remembering which objects that they have and have not counted.

Children also need to understand that they know how many things there are altogether from the last number said.

If you are counting objects, they can be counted in any order, and they can be moved around. There will still be the same number of objects!

With your child

- Where objects are in rows in the pictures, it is a good idea to encourage your child to count from left to right.
- Show them how to touch each object in turn as it is counted.
- Make sure that your child follows the rule of one object, one counting word.

Notes for Parents

Games to Play

Explanation

Playing games is the best way of helping your child
learn to enjoy numbers, to count and to recognise number shapes.

Your child will benefit from trying a variety of games. It is known that
learning through play is one of the best ways to develop early skills.

With your child

- Play counting games with your child using the pages in the book:
  Can you count …
    - ◆ two shoes – 'One, two'?　◆ three teddies – 'One, two, three'?
- Once your child is confident in this, look for smaller features of the pages:
    - ◆ Can you see three noses?　◆ Can you see four flowers?

- Every now and then there are 'mixed number' pages in the book.
  Use these to reinforce numbers already met, and to develop counting skills:
    - ◆ Can you find four butterflies?　◆ How many trees can you see?
- Turn to a new page and cover the large numeral with your hand.
  Challenge your child to work out what the numeral is by counting
  objects on the page.

- Reinforce the counting on the pages using actions:
    - ◆ Can you clap four times?　◆ Can you hop three times?

Recognising Numerals

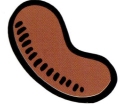

Explanation

As you come to each new page introduce your child to the numeral shape.

Explain that this is a way of showing the different numbers. We can show that there are six of something by drawing the numeral 6.

Use the number line which runs down the right-hand side of the pages. As you count down, draw attention to the numerals you reach. Make sure you do not say the next number until your finger has touched it.

Constant reinforcement like this will help your child to associate the number words with the numerals, or number symbols.

On each page you will also find the number word written in letters. Although your child may not be ready to read these, it is helpful to point them out.

With your child

- Trace over the large numeral shapes using a finger.
- Cut out some cards and number them 1 to 5. Make small collections of 1–5 objects and help your child to find the correct 'label' for each set.
- Draw a large numeral, e.g. 5, on a piece of card, and ask your child to draw five things around it.

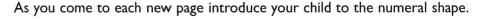

Numbers All Around Us

Explanation

It is important that your child learns that numbers are not just found in this book! The world is full of numbers and your child will see them everywhere you go.

Help your child to make connections between their everyday experiences and the book. For example:

'Here is a number 4. You will be 4 next time you have a birthday.'

Take opportunities to talk about numbers in everyday situations, encouraging your child to see that their new skills are useful.

With your child

- Draw attention to examples of numbers on road signs, car number plates, house doors or buses.
- Count the stairs as you climb them.
- Count items of clothing as you dress your child, especially shoes, socks and buttons.

- Count the numbers of items you buy when shopping or the number of objects used at mealtimes.
- Talk about numbers in the home:

  'We will need six spoons on the table at tea time.'

n o t e s

Rhymes and Songs

Explanation

Learning rhymes helps children to learn the order of number words which they will need for counting. Many rhymes involve actions, such as representing numbers using fingers. This is a great help in developing number recognition skills.

Most nursery rhymes and songs such as '5 speckled frogs' or '5 currant buns', count backwards. When you sing these songs it is a good idea to pause between verses and to count 'how many left', to remind children of the forward sequence of counting.

With your child

- Among the pages in the book you will find some examples of pictures which illustrate number songs:
  - ◆ Six fat sausages cooking in a pan,
    Sizzle, sizzle, sizzle, one went 'Bang!'.
  - ◆ Ten green bottles, hanging on a wall …
- Some number rhymes count forwards. For example:
  - ◆ One, two, buckle my shoe
  - ◆ 1, 2, 3, 4, 5,
    Once I caught a fish alive.

The Ten in a Bed Activity Page

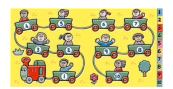

Explanation

This page can be used to encourage your child to count from left to right, touching each toy in turn.

Draw attention to the numerals from 1 to 10 and read them as you go to reinforce the sequence of counting words.

Match the numbers above the bed to those down the side of the page.

With your child

- Ask questions such as:
  - ◆ Which toy is number 3?   ◆ How many teddies can you see?
  - ◆ How many dolls?
- Talk to the children about the positions of the toys in the bed:
  - ◆ Which toy is next to number 10?
  - ◆ Which toy is between number 4 and number 6?
- Sing the song 'There were ten in a bed' with your child. Cover up the toys as you go to show how the number of toys gradually decreases during the song.
- Once your child is very confident in recognising numerals and knows their order well, play games in which you hide one of the numerals with a finger, and ask your child to guess which number you are hiding.

notes

... Notes for Parents

The Eggs in the Nest Activity Page

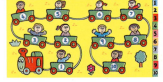

Explanation

This page introduces some of the early ideas of addition and subtraction, and gives you the opportunity to use some of the language associated with these.

With your child

- Start by counting the number of eggs in the nest in the first picture.
- Look at the second picture together. One of the eggs has hatched. There is one baby bird. Ask:
  - ◆ How many eggs are there now?   ◆ Are there more or less?

  Older children will be able to say that two is less than three, or three is more than two.
- Now look at the next picture. Another egg has hatched. There is one more baby bird. There is one less egg.
- In the last picture all three eggs have hatched. There are no eggs left. There is one more baby bird. There are three birds altogether.
- Give other counting challenges:
  - ◆ How many birds are there altogether?
  - ◆ How many eggs are there altogether?   ◆ How many nests?
- For older children, asking the question 'How many leaves can you see?' will introduce numbers beyond ten.

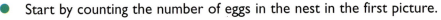
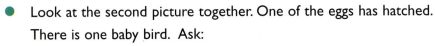
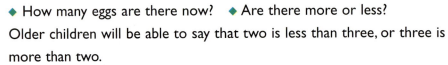
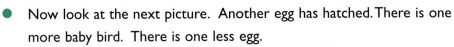